Fresh Wind

ISBN-13: 979-8685770882

LOC Control #: 2020908877

Copyright © 2020 and 2025 Cherie Sims

Publisher and Editor: The Beginning Publishing Company, LLC

This work was produced in Atlanta, Georgia, United States of America. All rights reserved under International Copyright Law. No portion of this publication may be reproduced, stored in any electronic system, or transmitted in any form or by any means (electronic, mechanical, photocopy, recording or otherwise) without written permission from the publisher or author, Cherie Sims. Brief quotations may be used in literary reviews. Unless otherwise noted, all scripture references have been presented from the New King James version or Amplified version of the bible.

Fresh Wind

By

Dr. Cherie Owens-Sims

Table of Contents

The Dedication

Thank You

The Family Blessing

The Foreword

The Introduction

Chapter 1: Receiving a Fresh Wind	27
Chapter 2: PUSH	33
Chapter 3: Finishing	39
Chapter 4: Breaking Point	45
Chapter 5: God Did It!	61
Chapter 6: All In	73
Chapter 7: Power	85
Chapter 8: Period	97
Connect with the Author	107

The Dedication

I want to thank my parents, Marshall and Emma Owens, for bringing me up in God and teaching me as a child how to trust and have FAITH in God and, most of all, how to pray. The Bible says in Proverbs 22:6, "Train up a child in the way he should go: and when he is old, he will not depart from it." I have learned that is such a true word from God. He knows what the future holds for each one of us.

I would like to thank my husband, Elder Lyndon Sims, for believing in me, and most of all, he believed in the God in me. Thank you for being my #1 supporter and pushing me to get this book out. He always said no matter what we are going through, "get the books out if you're tired of going through!" He was always willing to give up spending time with me so God's work could be done. Thank you so much for that support, bae.

To my children, thank you for always encouraging me to write my books. My #1 child, Armstrong, may your soul rest peacefully in heaven. Mama will see you again one day. To my #1 oldest daughter, Lady Lakesha Spears, my pastor, thank you for your constant support and push. To my #1 baby girl, gospel artist Kejuanna Owens, thank you for singing whenever I requested. To my #1 baby girl, Kaelyn Sims, thank you for praise dancing whenever I needed you.

I want to thank all of my siblings (my best friends) for your unconditional support of love shown one way or the other: Linda Dickens, Marsha Bond, the late Sandra Pennington (who has gone home to be with the Lord), Sharon Pace, Deondria Groves and my one and only brother, Darryl Owens. I am thankful for my few friends who have supported me along the way: Pastor Margaret Nutall, Latonya Gatson, Pastor Victoria Aggrey-Creppy, Pastor Teresa Battles, Collette Allen, Juanita Jeffries-Jackson, Pastor Nekisha Cosey & Monique Washington. I am thankful for my very own visionaries, Apostle PD and Pastor K (these two right here will support me to the moon and back).

I want to dedicate my first book, "Fresh Wind," to my mother, the late Mother Emma Johnson Owens. Thank you, Mama, for training me up in the Lord the right way as a child and teaching me how to fast, pray, and shut in with God. This will forever be with me and my children for the rest of our lives. With God's help, I vow to continue your family values. Your favorite saying, "God has never failed me yet." Amen and Amen! I dedicate this book to my mother-in-love, Mama Marie Carliss. Thank you for your support and encouragement.

I dedicate my eloquent way of dressing, boldness in speaking, preaching, and my strong FAITH to my grandparents, the late Rev. Ollie Johnson, and Mother Bernice Baker Johnson. Your Christian values continue on through your daughter, Patricia Adkins as she ends every prayer with Proverbs 3:6, "In all thy ways acknowledge Him, and He shall direct thy paths." Thank you, Aunt Pat.

I would like to also dedicate this book to my aunt, the late Mother Louise Owens, my spiritual mother. She taught me how to fight the devil back and not to be afraid. She taught me how to operate in the war room and because of that, I am now a called a demon chaser by my Pastors at World Shakers Ministries. She taught me how to smell when a demon was in the room. These POWERFUL people of God, my aunt, mom, and grandparents, have played some of the most important parts in my spiritual walk with God. Lastly, I dedicate this book to my daddy Marshall Owens. Even though you were not at church with us all the time, you liked preaching at home and you know the Word of God. You made sure we got up to go to church, Sunday Morning, Sunday Night, Tuesday, and Friday Nights. Staying home with you was not an option. Thanks for supporting mama as you both trained us in the right way to go. We love you so much because we know you wanted that for all of your kids. For that Daddy, I thank you. Mama is not here for the completion of my book, but I am so thankful that you are. Daddy with this book I have become the first author in our family, Dr. Prophetess Cherie Owens-Sims.

Thank You

To my graphic artist, Brion Dickens: You helped to bring the vision to life and produced something that was beyond my highest expectations! I appreciate you so much! THANK YOU!

To my Publisher, The Beginning Publishing Company, THANK YOU for every moment of encouragement and work dedicated to making this vision a reality.

The Family Blessing

~ To a woman with Fearless-Bold Faith,

Thanks for sharing and not being afraid to bring others on this faith ride with you - it shall make a difference in this world.

We are reminded of Ruth, a book of only four chapters. You are the fourth daughter born to Marshall & Emma Owens. Both you and Ruth have courageous faith, with a willingness to help others, and symbolize loyalty, devotion, and faithfulness. One lesson we have learned over and over again, through your faith, is that things are not always what they look like to us; God sees them differently than we see them. You have seen His work, time and time again, and He is good at what He does. You are a living testimony that He will do what He says He will do!

We have learned not to be so quick to judge and jump to conclusions. The way we see it, Ruth would never have gotten married. This same thought applies to you, as some of the things your faith has awarded you, our eyes would never have thought it would have come to pass. We do not know the end of our story; there is more to the story, to God be the Glory, but what we do know, it will be for our good.

Wishing you the Best,
Your Dad & Siblings

I am so happy for my beautiful and wonderful Mommy! I literally have watched her not only walk but live through and by faith all of my life! I am so grateful for the oil that resides on her and am so grateful that she would squeeze some of it out in this book. I watched her as a child pray and speak things without money or help from others, and it would happen because of a word from her mouth. I have so many stories - I remember one time a lady gave her a home and a dog because she spoke through faith into her life without fear! I remember witnessing that woman's testimony saying she was healed from cancer, and that touched me as a child; at that moment, I knew the power of FAITH. If I did not know anything else, one thing I was sure of is that I knew faith then, and I am who I am today because of the example my mother has been in front of her children - a Woman of Faith! Congratulations, my favorite girl. This book shall touch the nations.

With All Our Love,

Pastor Dennis and Lady Lakesha Spears

World Shakers Ministries

Duluth, GA

The Foreword

"Now Faith is the substance of things hoped for, the evidence of things not seen."

Hebrews 11:1

I was honored and excited when my friend Dr. Prophetess Cherie Sims asked me to write the forward of this wonderful book **Fresh Wind**. Reading the pages of the book, I note that it is all about faith. So, what Is faith? Faith is that spiritual force which opens humanity to a world of unlimited possibilities. Faith is a world of no limits, if you can believe, all things are possible, the scriptures say, "The just shall live by faith." Faith is a way of living and not a parachute used in case of emergency.

Faith is a lifestyle and not an event. It is how we live, as children of God, every day of our lives. Your life and ministry remain barren without faith. Faith is vital in your vision because without it you cannot get God to perform.

The word of God is delivered by faith. It is faith that gets the job done, not strength, effort or sweat.

Your vision can never deliver beyond the level of faith you are operating in. Faith is a spiritual chemistry; anytime faith is at work, a connection is established, which provokes the flow of virtue from God. In the story of the woman with the issue of blood (Luke 8:48) who touched the hem of Jesus' garment and was healed instantly, Jesus asked "who touched me?" Peter said to Him, "Master, the multitude throng and press you, and you say, 'who touched you?'

But Jesus said somebody touched me, for I perceived power (virtue) going out of me." (Luke 8:48 NKJV) In other words He said, "Somebody has tapped into what I carry, has connected with my virtue and has drawn out of me for a change of position!" Every time faith comes alive in any area of your life, you connect with divinity. Jesus said, "your faith has made you well." Faith is a" Living Force", drawn from the "Living Word", to produce "Living Proofs". Faith is the only way to move God in your direction. It is the only way to stop the devil. Faith is no cheap talk; faith is hard work (Hebrews 4:10-11) and requires a form of labor as you do not wish for faith but work at Faith.

We walk by Faith (2 Corinthians 5:7)

We take up the Shield of Faith (Ephesians 6:16)

We fight the good fight of Faith (1 Timothy 6:12)

We hold fast to the Profession of our Faith (Hebrews 10:23)

This book is tailor made to answer your questions and guide your Faith in God. Grab a copy; I know you will be blessed by it.

Rev. Mrs. Victoria Nana Creppy

First Lady and Co- Pastor

Grace Family International Church's

Founder of Women of Influence Talk Show

The Introduction

Fresh Wind is a book of faith, which has been lived out, walked out, talked out and preached out. This book contains real life truths. It is not based off lies, but instead, real life testimonies. That was witnessed by many people of God or revealed through the Word of God.

I was inspired by God to write this book of faith. It will show God-given powers in action and empower God's people all over the world, to believe, and trust, in Him for the impossible things that you cannot see, touch, or feel yet speaks, with such a volume that man's wisdom cannot comprehend. Fresh wind will empower you to push it out no matter how it turns up inside or outside. This written work will give you hope to live and strength to fight, to see what is in your next and make you believe in everything you once lost. You did not lose, but instead it was a win.

This book will teach us how to walk out into the light of God without worrying about whether you will fall or not.

It will deepen your understanding of what living by faith, and not by sight means. This is a book that will make you operate on such a level of faith that you did not even know you had it inside of you. It is all up to you how far you want to go to grow in your faith. This book will teach you that the sky is not the limit when you serve God. There are no limits or measures according to your faith. You do not have to start over – simply dust yourself off and get back to work. Whatever God call you to, learn to pray without ceasing. **Fresh Wind** teaches you that your faith operates like a system. It must be connected for it to work. That is called the belief system and is connected to the trust system and ultimately to the prayer system. It teaches you that the fivefold ministries are still going on and that it is time to push past negatively and birth out purpose, love joy and peace.

The bible says in Habakkuk 2:2-3 (KJV):

And the Lord answered me, and said, write the vision, and make it plan upon tables.

I wrote a long time ago that I am an author of many books, but I never did anything with it. This book will make you put your **FAITH** into action. It will encourage you to write, write, and write. It will help you to believe in the real you inside of **YOU**. It will give you every powerful reason to get your story out on paper or at the very least, push you in the right direction and teach you how we should be living through the operation of faith.

After reading this book, it is my prayer and declaration that you will find that your faith has increased to another level. You may be saying at this moment that you have not heard so much about faith or the ability for one to put It into action. <u>Fresh Wind</u> was written as a vehicle to let someone know that God is still moving in the supernatural, but the only way to truly grab hold of it is by stepping out into the deep by faith. Furthermore, this book will confirm that you are not crazy - you heard God, and you know it. This book is a reflection of what happens when you hear God speak and choose to obey immediately. The words in this book do not contain stories that have been heard, but the truth of God's Word lived out. I cannot wait for you to experience the power of God through the eyes of faith demonstrated in this book. Even as the author, it has increased my faith, and I trust that your testimony will echo the same.

Chapter 1

Receiving a Fresh Wind

Receiving a fresh wind will give you a different outlook on life. It will make you feel as if God really does hear you. Even in my darkest hour, right when I thought it was all over for me, God made me realize life has just begun. This is when I realized that a fresh wind does not come only because we go to church, because we know who God is or because my mother and father or grandparents raised us to know who God was. A fresh wind comes when you can trust God in everything you do.

Proverbs 3:5-6

In all thy ways acknowledge God in He will direct thy path. Trust in the Lord with all thy heart and lean not unto thine own understanding. and He will bring whatever your it is to pass.

Instantly this became a fresh wind, for you. When you begin to embark upon a fresh wind, it is then that your faith level must move to your next. In order to receive a fresh wind, you have to accept your current state. People will fight their current state because they do not know how to accept what is going on in the NOW of their lives, so they walk, around acting like they are being done wrong. Why? Because maybe we lost something along the way. It could have been a car, a house, finances or someone we loved dearly. It could even be something we loved very much like a relationship, a boyfriend or girlfriend or a result of divorce. We all have to learn how to let things go, in order to receive a fresh wind. Your fresh wind is what neutralizes all of your old losses and produces your win while you are going through. Even inside of your dry place, He will bring you out of that place when it feels like it is all over for you. It will make you smell the air you thought you never wanted to breathe again; this is where a fresh wind takes place.

When you begin to believe in your own heart that you have finally achieved the "big win" and refuse to lose any more to anything or anybody, the new you will emerge. Losing for me is never, ever, ever going to be an option ever again because I have faith in God, and I live and breathe God. If I am going to lose anything ever again, it will be by God's mandate alone.

We have the capacity and obligation to lose spiritual weight. Some of you have been carrying other people's problems for too long, but once you lose this weight, you will be free to move on to your next level in the things of God. You have to stop being a carrier! Satan constantly looks for a person or people who are willing to deliver the mail for him. Faith in God will kick the devil around! Faith is one of the most powerful tools you can carry. If you are going to be a carrier, trust me, you want it to be one of FAITH. Stepping out in faith brings out the warrior inside of you at any given time. It does not matter who you are, so make sure you stay prayed up, not laid up. FAITH will speak to you through void if you are willing to listen. FAITH is a driver - all you must do is step back and allow God to take the wheel. Having faith will produce many tears in your life, often becoming the kind you did not even know you could cry; they are called tears of unspeakable joy. "Now Faith", is a powerful word, all by itself.

I must take this moment to provide clarity for my readers that do not understand what faith really is, because they have never tried to operate in it until now because it hurt so badly. For some, it is called cancer, AIDS, sickness or brokenness. For others, you may know it as fire, prayer or becoming a fighter. It is powerful enough to make us believe that nothing can repair us but God and if God cannot do it, then it will not be done. There is nothing too hard for God, not even our worst mess. God has given us the ability to take back everything and anything the devil has stolen, from us; God is not going to come down and do this for us, but instead we have to decide on our own that we are going to trust Him no matter what. In season and out of season I still trust Him. It may look bad concerning my situation, but my answer is still yes.

Your faith must be set on fire through the unseen. Put your unseen operation in motion. It is finally time people of God to realize where and how you were slacking. If God gave you a tool that will make you rich or wealthy, then we as a people need to ask ourselves why we are not using it. He has given us the power to overtake every situation that stares us in the face. Decide today as you read this book that you are going to trust Him and refuse to be double-minded.

A double minded man is unstable in all his ways.

James 1:8

God wants us to stick to our faith and not waiver from it. If you trust God, do it in the good and the bad. If God did everything we wanted, when we wanted it, we would not be any good, not even for the kingdom.

God answers three ways—yes, no, or wait. We love the "yes," we hate the "no," and we do not have the patience to "wait" on God, so we keep getting ourselves in trouble that we cannot get out of unless God gets us out of it. To all my readers, take the pressure off because it can kill you, and believe me, that consequence is not worth it.

Chapter 2
Push

Push when that striking pain comes. Take a moment, inhale, breathe and push again. Push when you feel like you do not have the faith you need to get to your next level. People of God you must do the same exact thing you do when you birth a child, you push.

For the baby to come, you have to push. It may have given you a hard time, but it is ok; what it is not going to do is change the fact that you still have to push if you want to birth that baby. If it begins to hurt while you are pushing, we may have to stop the process, give you an epidural, and encourage you to step into that extra push through the place called ENCOURAGEMENT. We may even have to do surgery - cut you open to help you get that baby out headfirst, no matter how painful it gets. While stitching you back up, you still have to push your faith out, even if you have to deliver in the waiting room. Now that the baby is here, we have to take it out of your hands, clean it up, dry it off, and wrap it up. Why? Because new babies need to stay warm. Always keep your faith warm because you never know when or where you will use or need it. God's Word says you only need a grain, but I want to let you know that my voice is a "grain" and can move mountains all by itself. No matter how painful your situation, you still have to push. I know you may feel as if you are lazy and tired of trying, but to birth your new level in God, you must push. Some of you may have to push right away before something goes wrong.

Listen up! Get up and get some coffee because you are right where God wants you to be with your faith. The problem I am having with this whole scenario is this: you hear, read, and take in God's Word. You are jumping and shouting around on God's Word but refuse to have faith. Why sit there in pain when all you must do is push? I know this situation does not look like what you imagined, so you refuse to push because your inside wants it to look like it will not hurt. I cannot tell you your push is not going to hurt, but I can promise you that it is going to be the beginning of something new. Once you push and your brand-new level begins, you have to clean up all the old mess and celebrate your new life with tender, loving care. When God gives you a new level of faith, you must be careful with it, how you handle it, your surroundings, and who and what you expose it to.

It is your job to dress your new baby, clothe and feed it, nurture and train it in the way you want it to grow. Your faith can grow, big, long, little or small, wide, deep, or maybe not. If you do not use your faith and water it, you will never be able to measure it. You need at least a grain of mustard seed for this baby I keep talking about to grow. Sometimes, you have to quit whatever you are doing if you do not see any growth in your walk with God. Doing a walkthrough down memory lane is okay to see if there have been any changes in your life. If nothing has changed, start over! People do it all the time, baby after baby, until they get what want. Sometimes they were not expecting the blessing but because they were in the right place at the right time they still got blessed. Sometimes you have to babysit yourself, watch over your own gifts and not allow any bad spirits around it until it develops to a place where it can grow. Spreading your faith can go as far as you can believe! The sky is not your limit - faith has limits you do not even know about. God said in His Word that He gives it out according to what measure you have. If you do not have any faith at all, purchase some because in order to please God you have to be able to measure it. Without faith, it is impossible to please Him. You should always pray to be pleasing to God in his eyesight. Do not always run and tell somebody what God is doing with your new. Stop telling everyone how it works; you are still learning yourself.

Some of you have been saved all your life but have never stepped out on faith. Your mother did it for you! Your

Father did! Your grandparents did it! Despite their strides, you never experienced it and are still living off your connection. Now the lights are flickering, and you do not know what to do because your parents and grandparents are gone. Your lifeline connection is gone and now you have to give birth yourself and learn the hard way. Stop putting what you birth out of faith in the wrong hands. What you worked so hard for, prayed so hard for and fasted so long for is now stolen because you put it and the wrong hands, wrong ears or possibly the wrong inbox.

Chapter 3

Finishing

We must complete whatever we start, but you have to start first in order to finish. I have never seen anyone finish anything; as a matter of fact, they never started. Always make sure you stay inside your lane. Once you start, it is just like a race you were winning when you started because you stayed in your lane. The rules are as follows: You can only finish what you start in your own lane. If, for some reason, you end up in the wrong lane, it is your fault. After all, you decided to help somebody else win because you disliked your lane. Now, you have to wait until the next race comes again so that you can try again. The bible says:

"You ran well but who hindered you."

-Galatians 5:7

You cannot point the finger at anybody but yourself. There is no one to blame it on. Trust me, you do not want to complete someone else's assignment. Use whatever you have on your life to accomplish the destiny set before you. God equips us all with some great tools, but we do not like how ours works for some reason, so we want to borrow someone else's anointing. It looks like what God wants us to do is boring, but what He has for you will be so much more beneficial. Finish it even when you do not feel like being the finisher.

Many times, we fill up when we are almost at the finish line because we cannot see with our own eyes that we are almost there; it feels like it is taking such a long time. No matter how we try to see it, we do not see it. We cannot put our hands on it; we try really hard to believe, but we always give up because it looks like, or should I say, it is taking everything out of us to finish.

We must have faith even when we are not able to see it being finished our way. In this walk of life, in order to finish, you are or will have to trust in THE FINISHER 100 percent. Again, I say, "you ran well but who did hinder you" or shall I say, "what did you allow to hinder your belief system?"

You have to believe in your start. You cannot get in the middle of the race and quit; you must remember you are in this race to win. It does not matter who finishes first. You may fall along the way, but the bible says a young man **"will fall seven times but get back up." (Proverbs 24:16)** These are God's words, not mine. Dust your dirty knees off and try again and again and again and never give up. As long as you have breath in your body you keep on trying; like the battery, it keeps on going and going and going to keep running the race. If you get tired along the way, take a five-minute break, keep watering it and keep running. If a runner had known they were going to fall before they ran the race, they would not have run, but they went into the race blinded, just knowing in their heart they were in it to win. Your aim should be to win no matter what or how hard the race is. Just like your faith walk, your aim should be to win. No matter what it takes, you started trusting God and should not change your mind now. Just because someone got ahead of you does not mean you lose.

The process should not make you stop. You must believe in your heart that the race is not over just because you are not finished. It should encourage you to keep on in the faith race, knowing that you are doing something right. You still have a chance to win because of God's timing. Your win is not dependent on man's time. As long as you have breath inside your body, your faith race is not over until

God says it is over. What God has for you it is for you. Nothing and nobody can stop that. Nobody can take it because God designed it just for you. According to the measure of your faith makes you one of God's custom designs. You are one of God's faith celebrities. Walk around in your new from now on because you can go as far as you will allow your FAITH to take you. Somebody is saying, "is it just for me?" The bible says,

"Eyes have not seen, ears have not heard, neither has it entered in the heart of man the things that God has prepared for you."

1 Corinthians 2:9

For the designer pieces who love the Lord, your faith can be like a yo-yo; it goes up and it goes down. It is according to the measure you have. Everybody's faith is different; it is not measured the same. Faith comes in different size packages. What size is your faith? All you need is a grain but be honest with yourself: Is that all you want, a mustard seed? If you are a new believer, this book is a great starting place. Sometimes, when wondering what is wrong with our FAITH systems, I conclude that we have been carrying seeds of the same size for a long time. Some of you are okay with what your size seed can move, but imagine if you had greater FAITH than what you already possess? What would your life be like if you had greater faith than what you are settling for? Your faith can make all your impossible situations possible. You do not have to see it in order to believe it, but some of you do not know how to trust God unless you can see everything.

Stop immediately and repent so God can forgive you and bless your efforts.

Chapter 4

Breaking Point

Sometimes in your life, you reach the breaking point and say, "Lord, I cannot do this marriage anymore! I cannot do this job! I cannot do this relationship anymore. It looks like nothing is happening for me!" Even when it seems that everything is happening for everyone around you, at some point, you have to say in your mind, "I am going to trust God no matter what my situation!" There comes a time in your life when you have to stop allowing life's problems to break you down because, really, if it breaks you, it will stress you out, which is unhealthy. Trust me, it is not what you want. Stress will cause many problems, such as headaches, heart problems, etc. You do not have to look for them; it is an automatic problem. Stress will come for you through bill collectors, families, and other issues — relationships, friendships, work, and even church problems. That is exactly why the bible says,

"When I go to do good evil is always present."
Romans 7:21

Your FAITH will hold you up when you feel like there is nothing left. Always remember that God will not put more on you than you can bear. Ask yourself this question: Why are you telling God you cannot handle it? God is looking down at you, saying, "Yes, you can handle it because My Words will not go out and come back void! I promised in My Word that I will not put more on you than you can bear!" It gets hard when you consistently look at the situation; trust God to navigate you through your faith walk. It is a blinded thing, so you must allow God to navigate your walk of faith. God said if you are going to step out and trust His Word, you must step out believing that. When stepping out on His Word at any given time, that God -

word will find you right where you are because we know that God's word always stands, and it speaks with volume.

I remember looking for a house in 1992, and I did not have a clue as a woman of faith what God was up to. I made an appointment to see a house; the landlords gave me a time to come see it. When I got there, it was a husband and a wife, and I remember thinking to myself, "This is a beautiful house!" I wondered why they were leaving the house, so I approached the landlord and asked, "Can I ask you a question?" She replied, "Sure!" I said, "This house is beautiful! Why are you letting it go?" She explained to me that though she loved her house, her husband was sick with cancer, the doctor was giving him up, and he was about to go to the cancer institute. How many know that God is at the cancer institute? I asked her if I could pray for her husband. I told her that I was a prophet and that I honestly believed that my reason for being inside her home was to pray for her husband.

I asked her, "Do you believe in God? She said, "Yes!" I asked, "Do you believe God can work miracles?" She said, "Yes!" I asked her, "Can I pray for your husband right now, here in this living room? She said, "Yes!" I told her that God wanted to heal him, and if they believed, he could be healed right then in the mighty name of Jesus. She said she believed it, so then I turned to her husband. I asked him, "Sir, do you believe that God can heal you?" He said, "Yes!" I asked him, "Do you mind if I pray for you?" He said, "No," so he began to pray right there in the middle of his house inside the living room while other people were walking through the house. I really did not care because I am a firm believer that God takes the foolish things to confound the wise. I began to pray off that old ugly spirit called cancer, binding it up down on earth and heaven, and sealed that prayer in Jesus' name. I began to ask the man if he believed that God could heal his little situations. He said, "Yes!" I asked God to heal this man. I said, "God, I hold You to Your Words, not mine. Your Word says that by

Your stripes we are healed. If your word is true to heal this man of God, I ask that you make a true believer out of him right in this living room so that he can know exactly who you are!"

I told the man, "I am here to look at your house, for what I really do not know because I just bought my first beautiful house five minutes away from you. I really was just doing something and decided I would look for a bigger house, and here I am, but God did that. You had been praying to be healed, so to God, the foolish thing was your house being put in a newspaper for rent and allowing me to fall in love with this house to get me to you." The truth about this whole situation is that God wanted this man to know who God was and who he belonged to.

God heard his prayers because he prayed, asking God to heal him. God told me to tell the man, "You are healed right now in Jesus' name." I told the man, "Yes, I wanted this house, but if I never get this house after this, as long as God heals you, I will be fine. I will give up this house to see you healed. It does not matter, one way or the other, as long as you are healed, I will be fine." They said they would get back to me and let me know whether I got the house or not, so I agreed and said, "I know this is my house. I will be waiting to hear from you guys." I also told her to take my phone number because even if I did not get the house, I wanted to hear the official news about how God healed him.

Two weeks went by, and I never heard back from them. I knew it would take a while to receive the update because he was on his way to the cancer institute. Whose report are you guys going to believe? I am going to believe the report of the Lord! No matter what, in every one of my situations, I believe God's Word will not fail but it will speak, and when it speaks it sounds the loud alarm that once again, God did it. Suddenly after not hearing from them for a very long time, I got a phone call. I said,

"Hello." She said, "Is this Cherie?" After confirming, she said, "This the lady that you met a while back. You prayed for my husband when you came and applied for the house." I said to her, "How did things go?" She told me that everything went great and thanked me for praying for her husband. She then let me know that **MY** new house key was under the mat by the back door. After that, I never heard from or saw them again. I remember giving them $2,000 and paying rent the following month and not knowing how to contact them anymore for anything. They just gave me the house and every now and then she would call and tell me hello, but I never really heard from them again in my life. They just gave me the house as God instructed them and moved on. Now this to me was a fresh wind putting my faith in action. The big picture right here is that God was trying to show us that He will bless us if we trust Him; there a blessing tied up in being obedience. A fresh wind comes when you are walking around in victory. Yes victory!

I remember another time I was really feeling sick in my body. I went to the emergency room. At the time, I was living at 1309 Old Country Circle, which was the first home I ever purchased. My "EX" and I (yes, I said, "EX" husband") had started a church in our garage. I got sick and went to the hospital. I felt good the entire day, but around 9pm, I began to feel sick. The nurse came in and told me I had a two-hour wait. I asked her if I could sit in the waiting room so I would not be alone. She said yes. There was a very pretty old lady sitting in the waiting room. I said "hello," and she spoke back. I said, "Can I ask you a question?" After she gave me permission, I asked her why she was there, and she told me because she had cancer. I asked her if she knew God. She said, "Yes, I pray to God all the time, but He has not helped me." I told her, "That's not true. That is a trick of the devil!" I told her, "I believe God so much! He sent me here just to talk to you! I'm not able to sit anymore since I have been talking to you." I told her I was a true prophet, and God had a Word for her.

She said to me, "I hope so prophet because the four doctors I just got through seeing a few minutes ago told me to go home, call all my kids and tell them they can be on their way, and now you're telling me God sent you here for me!" She said, "What church do you attend? Give me the address!" I gave her the address and she told me she would visit that Sunday.

She drove for about an hour to come and visit us. Sunday came and the doorbell rang. The kids opened the door, and the lady said, "Do y'all have a church call True Believer in FAITH service?" After they confirmed, she said that she was there to see me, so they let her in. The church was packed. She smiled and waved as she entered the church and sat in the front row. The church service was so good that Sunday - the praise and worship was relentless - the choir was phenomenal. She got happy and then the pastor asked if anyone had a testimony. She raised her hand with three other people and said out loud, "Yes I have a testimony!" The devil began to speak to me saying, "She's coming to tell them you are not a true Prophet," but I told the devil where he could go. She pointed me out and said real loud to the crowd: "I met y'all First Lady at the hospital last week as we were sitting in the waiting room, and I told her I had stage four cancer, that the doctors had given me up, and told me to contact my kids. She told me she was a prophet and that God had sent her to the hospital just for me. She came to tell me that I would live and not die and that I did not have cancer in my body. I came today to tell her I had called my doctors, and all four of them had set me up for more testing. I want to say to her today in front of all her church that I go back to the hospital for a test next week to check me out, and if they say I have cancer. I will be back to tell y'all that this woman of God is a fake prophet, and if they cannot find any cancer. I will be back to tell y'all that this woman of God right here is not only a true prophet, but she is on point, and God really does use her. Not only that, but I will also move out of my $3,000 per month house and give it to the prophet, the true woman of God." The church saints got quiet. The pastor began to preach but church just was not the same after Mrs. Johnson stepped in.

Sunday service was over, and the "time of fellowship" began. Everybody started laughing and hugging. One of the members asked me what I was going to do if that lady stopped her family from coming and she finds out she is still dying from cancer. I told her, "You sound crazy! God said she was healed, and she will live and not die. That's not my problem! She will just have to wait on God." About four to six weeks went by and every time the church doors opened, I looked to see if it was her and everyone else was looking too. It came to a point when we all stopped looking for her to come through that door. My ex - husband asked me, "Do you think she is coming back?" I responded with the most confident "yes" that I could release. He then said, "Why you think she is coming back?"

I continued, "I told her to bring me the keys to my new house and to testify that I am a true prophet in front of all the haters and naysayers." God will bless you right and front of your enemy's face (you better ask somebody!)

We were into about weekend number six that Sunday morning, and everything was going slowly. The church was full to the max and service was going to its next level of praise. I was praising God to the highest. The church door opened, and it was the lady. All I remember is that the church went from high praise to complete quietness, and everyone was looking at me. I began to smile, and I waved at Mrs. Johnson. She did not smile back; at that time, the devil tried to speak in my ear, yelling, "Everybody's going to find out that you are a fake prophet today." I told that old devil that what they were going to find out was that God rules. Service had already started, and then the Pastor asked, "Does anybody have a testimony?"

Mrs. Johnson said, "Yes, I have a testimony, Pastor."

Everything stopped immediately — that is how the devil is. They were all waiting to hear that lady say that after seeing four doctors the word I gave her was wrong and that I was a fake prophet, but how many of you know if you wait on God to develop your gift it will have authentic results? So, Mrs. Johnson got up to tell her testimony and began it with a frown on her face. As I was waiting, I remembered saying in my mind, "Come on God! Show these people how you work."

She said, "The woman of God said I would live in, not die. Like I told y'all before, I'm a woman of my word. I told you all that if I got checked by these doctors. They said that I still had cancer, I was coming to tell y'all that she is a fake prophet, but if they did not see cancer, she would be a true prophet, and I would bring her the keys to my house. When I was here the last time, I also told her that I was a Baptist and I was going to stay a Baptist, but today I want to tell y'all!" Immediately, she fell to the floor and began speaking in tongues. I remembered watching the church look a little disappointed because there were some that I knew wanted to hear some bad news. She got up, barely able to stand, and said, "Y'all have a true prophet in this house! This girl came to the hospital to tell me I was healed. I called and told my kids that they did not have to come, and now I'm here to bring her the keys to her new house, and you can have the dog too. I already moved into my apartment. Here go your keys!" We completed the transaction the next day with the banks and completed all the paperwork. God stands on His word! He will show up and show out. People did not understand at first because some of them told me, "I'm not going to lie; with that look on her face, I just knew she was coming to tell you that she still had cancer, but not one time did you pay attention to the way she was looking. It was as though you knew God would not fail you!"

Chapter 5

God Did It!

With confidence on my face and my mother's words, I am typing this at fifty-seven years old, God has never failed me! I have never prophesied, and it has not come to pass. If you are a true prophet and God speaks through you for real, it will not be a question as to who you are. God will prove if they are a true prophet or if it was not God. Everyone is not a prophet, and real prophets do not even want to be prophets.

Let me give you one more faith testimony – it is going to be a real shift and right to the point. I was told that God was going to bless me with my own house when I moved back to Milwaukee. I believed it; I hated staying in that little apartment building after living in my 3,000-square-foot house in Georgia and owning two more nice houses I was renting out. I found a house, and when I pulled up, I said, "No way! It's a little bittie, but I am still going inside because the owner is expecting me." I walked inside and could not believe what I saw - it was a beautiful four-level home. Long story short, I lived there paying $1,350 a month for a year and a half, and then for the next fourteen days, I did not have to pay a dime. I closed on the house in 1997, and they even gave me $10,000 after the closing with no down payment. I got a divorce in 1999, had not paid rent, and had six years left with $15,000 in taxes from my former marriage. In the year 2000, I took out an equity loan to open a new company for $30,000. I used $10,000 to open my daycare and paid the $15,000 taxes off. I tried to return the house, but he said he did not want it back. He signed the whole mortgage over to my name. The house was already paid for the day I moved. This testimony shows us all that your faith must accompany your belief system and that it is measured according to you.

Here is a bonus testimony just for you: In 2002, I moved out of the little house that I loved because I got a phone call asking if I wanted a bigger house. I said "yes" right away because I began listening to friends tell me I needed a bigger house and that my current one was too small. I had just remodeled my house - sky windows, floors, carpet, glass double doors, new cabinets, slide doors, and even cut some walls open. Six months later, the phone call about my next move came. I left my newly remodeled house and moved into a big house; I went from paying nothing to $1,000 a month. I soon discovered that the whole basement was molded! Then, a friend told me that the home was too small, so I moved to a beautifully made house in River Hills (that name was big back then), paying $3,500 per month. It was not my house; instead, I was renting from a friend. That did not work out, so I ended up living at an Extended Stay for the first time ever in my life. While going through a fight concerning it in court, one of my sisters said, "God said go buy you your own house!" I did not think that I could because by this time I had filed chapter 7 and two chapter 13 bankruptcies. Years went by, I never checked my credit. After inquiring, I discovered that my credit score was 750, so I applied for a house. They approved me right away! I began to think, "if God said go buy me a house and I want a $500,000 home, God said it is so!" Not only did God do it, but I walked away with $10,000!

Faith does not have any kickstand; when you stop having it, you just stop having it. If you feel like you do not trust or believe God like you once did, then you should reach out, pray to God and ask Him to renew your spiritual eyesight. Tell Him that you want to be better! When it comes to trusting God, if I develop a prayer life through that type of power my faith walk with God will kick back in.

Whatever is inside of you will speak; if your heart is full of doubt that is all that will come out of you, but if it is full of power, that will come out instead. That "full of life faith" must be enabled while you walk in God. It is just like the electric company - you believe if you pay your electric bill that the lights will stay on but if you do not pay the bill, your lights will go out and you will be in the dark. Once you get to this place, you must pray, believe and trust God to make a way. Well, the same thing applies to your faith: if you let the light go out, you will have to pay the bill in order for the faith lights to come back on; we walk by faith not by sight.

    We pay our bills by repenting and praying, asking God to forgive our unbelief, and telling Him that we will try to trust Him and believe Him with all we have. After that, we make a decision and pursue the path of keeping our prayers going because they are the lighter fluid for our faith. It fires up our belief system; that is when we are filled with the power and authority required to call out demons, heal the sick, opening the blind man eyes and raise the dead. Faith can cancel things like AIDS, cancer, strokes, lies, poverty and yes, fear too. You must believe against the odds with your faith; when the devil says "no" your faith speaks with volume and says "yes!" Faith says,

"I can do all things through Christ who strengthens me."
Philippians 4:13

Faith can move that big old mountain out of your way. Faith is a carrier of the Word that you are approved. Faith goes before judges and changes your sentence. Faith opens jail doors - look at Paul and Silas! They prayed until the jail cells opened! That is how powerful their prayers were; and because they believed that their prayers would touch God, He answered. Their prayers released them from their imprisonment. The guard was on duty but in a deep sleep. They could have hurt him, locked him up or made fun of him but they did not do that; instead, they began to praise God for the act of faith that he had performed. That would not have happened if they did not believe it! I trust God even more after reading this, how about you? One lesson to be learned in this is there is nothing too hard for God or too big. Your big situation is a little thing to our big God. His words say:

"Without faith it is impossible to please Him."
                                                    Hebrews 11:6

We should all strive to be pleasing in God's sight. Starting out with now faith is the substance of the stuff we are asking God for, and the evidence is when we see it or feel it (Hebrews 11:1). Even when we do not have a clue or know when it is going to happen, we continue to trust God through the process.

Despite the tears in your eyes, you still must keep your yes! You may be homeless but keep your yes! You may have lost a loved one, but keep saying yes! Even if you are talked about, tell God yes! No matter what, keep your yes! As you continue to confess with your mouth and worship Him, sooner or later, He will send a fresh anointing your way, and you will experience a fresh wind from Him. As you keep reading this book, I pray that a cloud begins to form right where you are and that you realize that God designed this book just for you. It is your time. The wait is really over for you. God just had to boost your faith back up. Your life will never be the same after you read this book. There is such an anointing being released that will empower you and enlighten your path. You are walking in the Lord. If you started out with just a mustard seed of faith after receiving this fresh wind, you will begin to feel God breathing on you. Your life will never ever be the same. You will begin to feel like the dead things inside of you are moving around and waking up, and at that very moment is where you will realize where you left your faith. You will realize where you left your joy; it has been in the waiting room this entire time.

I felt like I was getting too old for the promises of God. I began to believe the feelings I had inside of me, and I shut down the possibilities. I stopped praying about it along the way. I did not see it coming because I never stopped serving God (at least that is what I said, but after writing this book, I really did stop serving God.) I had to repent to God and myself because I failed us both. That is why I love God so much - He never fails. I thought and felt like it was all over for me, but after writing and reading this book, I realize that I am just getting started. God just had me set aside for such a time as this. Now, I am praying and laying prostrate before the Lord and trust me, it is waking up the things I thought were dead inside of me. Just like Martha and Mary, they were friends with Jesus. They walked with Him and had the best of Him. They were close to Him, but when their brother Lazarus died, they sent for their friend Jesus, and he did not come when they sent for Him. In fact, He waited a couple of days! They did not like being in the waiting room when they knew Jesus had the power to save their brother. Jesus decided to come a couple days later. They blamed Lazarus' death on Jesus, saying:

"If You had been here, Lazarus would be alive."

John 11:21

Like some of us, we blame everything we are going through on God - our ups, downs and everything in between. We refuse to have faith, believe the Word of God and trust God. So now, we want to throw in the towel saying, "God allowed us to go through like this! I feel like a curse is on me! Why can't God stop this pain!" Just like Martha and Mary, they should have known who God was and what He could do; then they really could have gotten some rest and confidently said, "When God shows up, He will get him up!

He is just resting!" Despite the hope, their faith was not big enough for them to believe like that.

CHAPTER 6

All In

Like some of us, our faith may need to move to the next level because what you believe with may not be able to move this mountain; you have to add more. Some things only come out by prayer and fasting (Matthew 17:21). Fasting, praying, believing, and trusting God is the answer sheet to pass the test. Some people feel that because they lose things along the way, they are better off serving the devil. Not so! God wanted us to see the big picture. Your lesson does not always come when you have evidence of His presence; it comes when you cannot see, feel, or find Him but can still trust and believe that He will never leave you nor forsake you, said the Lord. Jesus returned and went to the grave, calling Lazarus' name and telling him to "come forth" and Lazarus arose from the dead. All God wanted was for us to move in faith and to declare things that are not as though they are. You must believe that once you receive the real Holy Ghost, He will lead and guide you to all paths of righteousness.

I call forth the prayer warrior! I call forth the prophet! I call forth healing! I call forth five-fold. I decree and dismiss doubt, fear, abuse, hate, anger, and jealousy. Remember, it is not over until God says it is over. Lord, let Your fresh wind breathe on us over and over again until we get ourselves together! I pray that your prayer, FAITH, belief, and trust systems connect and reach levels you cannot even imagine. You have to say to yourself, after reading this book, "I'm going to come out of this!"

Lord, I thank You for the makeover You gave us through this fresh wind. I ask You now, Lord, to allow the Holy Ghost to embark upon us as we step out into this wicked world using the measure of faith that You have given us to compare and release the benefits that come along with faith. Lord, we thank You for a fresh wind that will blow out of Your mouth like fire as we speak the Word of faith! We tell Satan to get thee behind us! We will succeed in the things of God. We are winners and never losers. My circle is winning! My family is winning! Everything connected to me is winning! From now on, they win! When the doctors say "no," God says, "Yes, we win!" We refuse to take any more losses - all we accept are strong wins. When the bank accounts are empty, we still win because it is in the emptiness that God can give us a fresh wind and show Himself. I win, you win, they win because our faith has made us eligible to be on the winning team!

Jesus was a great example of a fresh wind: they hung Him high; they stretched Him wide; He hung His head and then He died but that had to take place in order for us to receive our fresh wind. On that third day He promised us He will rise again, and He did just that! You too are going to rise again, and you are going to be smarter and brighter. Yes, believe it! The spirit of God inside of you will not die, cannot die and you will rise again. The bible says,

If I abide in You and you abide in Me, you can have anything you ask according to the word and I will give it to you.

John 15:7

Do me a favor: stop wherever you are, pause for a moment and ask God to let the dead inside of you rise. Now that you have asked such a great and easy thing for God to do, you have to protect all of your connections to your faith system. With everything you have inside of you, do not leave your faith unprotected. Always keep it covered; this is the key.

One way to protect your faith is through prayer. Prayer moves doubt to its own brand-new location. It moves unbelief around to the same place (hold on, unbelief needs a ride!) Prayer neutralizes the attack; it stops the process the devil has set up for you. When the devil is targeting you, your prayers shut it down. Faith is a power pill; it comes out and burns up every lie against you. It gives favor you did not earn or deserve. It fights the fight of faith for you. It tears up all the tension in the room. It works miracles that will make men's disbelief system change its mind (i.e., good health, a prosperous life, favor of God, and your entire family winning!) This is the evidence of things that may not have been seen before but can become your reality now. I encourage you to fast and believe! As you trust God to give you a fresh anointing and to put you back on the potter's wheel to make you usable again, tell God, "I'm tired of fighting! I receive my fresh wind! I am getting up and getting out of the rut I have been in. I am speaking and declaring that I will glow in my season, for my life is now ready to receive a fresh wind from You!"

God will love you more in the waiting room. Just because you are in the waiting room, that does not mean that God does not love you. Instead, it means that God loves you so much that he refused to allow you to continue in your mess, so He stopped the process. God desires to make us over again, but instead of trusting Him we would rather hear it through man. God Himself desires to put us back on the WHEEL and make us all over again; this is how much God loves us - enough to stop us in our tracks and make us all over again. Your faith will raise up and speak for you. I am free! I am whole! I am somebody! I am taking over the land. God has given us dominion and power. In this world, you have to speak life over yourself and what and who ever you are connected to.

I will live and not die.
I will not be broken.
I will never receive sicknesses on myself nor my family — it is not of God.
I will not bury another family member before their God given time.
I am a winner, even when it looks like and feels like I am losing.
I still speak a win out of my mouth.
Life and death is in the power of my tongue.
I will get back on track and I believe that God will go before me every time. He will be there every step of the way.

I have the faith that when I go to possess the land that God will go before me.

Every witch and warlock that comes up against me, God will fight from now on no matter what battle it is.

God will approve everything I ask Him for, as it is in His divine plan and will.

God will stop and block the enemy that throw fiery darts against me and what is connected to me. I will conquer everything I set out to do!

If I can believe it, I can achieve it even when I cannot see it!

I affirm that the unseen God is like scotch tape in my life - I cannot see Him but will trust Him over and over and over again!

God always keeps His word concerning us. He will never leave us nor forsake us. We are the ones that do not keep our word when it comes to God. How can you not trust a God like this? He grants us a fresh wind every time, but for some reason, we keep falling back into the same old mindset every round. Yes, I said round because FAITH is like boxing

- you have to put on your boxing gloves if you plan to win. You have to start fighting that old devil back for what you believe in. Just because you lose two or three rounds does not mean you are not winning. It is called "gains through loss;" sometimes, God wants us to lose because it will teach us how to have patience. All losses are not permanent. Sometimes, patience with God will teach us to fall back on our knees and worship God. Operating in FAITH one or two times does not give you enough for a lifetime. You have to keep storing it. Faith cannot and will not be erased; it leaves behind testimonies every time. Faith allows you to make history every time you tell of God's goodness. It makes others step out into their next. How about you? This time around, ask God to give you a fresh anointing! Speak into the atmosphere!

I am moving in faith! From now on, I will pay my tithes.

Malachi 1:8

Let's consider this:

Study to shew thyself approved unto God, a workman that needeth not to be ashamed, rightly dividing the word of truth.

2 Timothy 2:15

Receive the blessing of that scripture! Not only that, He also said,

"and I will rebuke the devourer for your name sake!"

Malachi 3:11

You have to believe you cannot and will not beat God's giving no matter how you try. You have to stop fighting against your faith and level up. Level up in your giving and do the right thing! Level up in your faith walk. Level up and admit you need to be delivered! If you are going to receive a fresh wind you must shift and level up! The secret is giving! Pay your tithe and sow your offering! If you do not pay them, the bible says you are cursed with a curse (Malachi 3:9) and no man can remove that curse but God.

Through your prayers and repentance, He will forgive you. Pray along with me:

Dear Lord,

I know that I have not paid my tithes like I should. I really do not have any excuse because I believe if I give all my excuses up and believe in your Word, You will hear my heart, one of true repentance, and forgive me.

CHAPTER 7

Power

You have to come clean with God no matter what.

He is not a man that he will lie neither the son of mat that he shall repent.

Numbers 23:19

God already knows what angle you are coming from, so why not just ask God for forgiveness and ask Him to make you better. Ask Him to put you back on the wheel! Allow God to remove the curse. I believe God forgave, us how about you? It is according to the measure of our faith. Where you go next depends on what you can believe or want to believe; God left it all up to us. It is all connected to our belief system.

When you level up and begin to live right and do the right thing concerning God's word, you get access to the throne and the ability to ask whatever it is you want, but know this, if you decide to make your bed in heaven God is there, and hell, God is there. So, with that being said, if you want a fresh wind in God, you have to level up and come clean, so together, let us repent of the known and the unknown so we can level up, grow up, and embrace our new. The 2020 fresh wind is going to escort us into the year 2021 with a new connected lifeline. It is time to trust God, read your Bible, and fight spiritually! Move in silence! A fresh wind will give you the ability to level up in every area of your walk with God. It will encourage you to study even more.

I thank God for all the wonderful readers who took time out of their busy schedules to bless and experience a fresh wind in their lives one way or another. I am praying and hoping that every word in this book will inspire someone's faith and soul to catch on fire and step into their next level or dimension of faith. When fear comes to knock on your door telling you all of those lies, you have to send FAITH to answer all of your fears! When the devil targets you to talk about you, pick on you, or trouble you, believe that God is promoting you to the next level! Level up, soldiers! This army you have enlisted in requires you to be prepared to fire back with God's word. When you can go through everything you have been through and still find a YES deep down in your soul for the miracle you have been preparing for, you must know that you are closer to your prize.

Do not birth Ishmael in the waiting room - move higher! Now that you have received your fresh wind, it is time to move up the ladder. I need you to begin to reach for your next. Grab it, and do not let it go! God will stop the troubling of the waters for you, and anything that comes trying to stop you will be thrown overboard. Get far away from it! From now on, throw doubt overboard! Throw fear overboard! Throw backbiters overboard. Throw "hearsayers" overboard! Throw liars overboard! Thrown hate overboard! Throw every contrary situation overboard! Now, it is time to welcome positive vibes into your world, which is a part of the faith system. Welcome love, life, and fresh anointing! Take faith with you inside your wallet, purses, car, to work, and yes, even the grocery store, church, and the mall. Faith is everywhere you go if you choose to believe it; faith without works is dead, so you have to work on your faith!

Listen! The waters are coming down, the leaves are blowing, and a fresh wind coming your way. For every reader, cherish every moment. God is giving you a fresh wind; it may beat up on the walls of your belief system, but if you stay prayed up, it can only bless you. As the fresh wind blows, it causes everything the devil set up for you to fail. Readers, please trust God - the beat goes on with or without you. Continue to move strong; somebody has to win and lose. There will always be somebody new standing in line trying to receive what you refuse to accept, but the beat still goes on. It is just like fishing in the ocean - there will always be a new catch, just like this fresh wind. Discover yourselves through believing the unseen; eyes have not seen, ears have not heard, nor has it entered into the hearts of man the things God has prepared for those who love the Lord. In all your ways, acknowledge God, and He will direct your path.

Discover your inside gifts! The Bible says to stir up the gifts that are inside of you. As you stir up your gifts, you will discover something about yourself that you did not know. You really do not even know what is really inside of you until you begin to stir it up. You may find a Preacher, Teacher, Prophet, Evangelist, or Apostle. We do not know, but you may even find a server! It is all connected to your faith system according to what you believe; if you believe you have a winner inside of you, people of God, stir it up and allow your fresh wind to come. Once you stir it up, you have to come out working. You have to first try before you give up.

People who have not tried to live in faith will oftentimes give it up, but it is worth a try, trust me. When you have tried everything else, why not trust, believe, and try the best thing that God gave us - our faith and belief system? Your faith is just like stairs and steps - you have to believe it can hold you up at all times. If you can trust God and step out, He will always make a way. Your faith is an outlet; for whatever you want and need from God, you have to learn that when all else fails, faith will stand up in the midst of failure. Faith is a positive - it always overrides the negative! Faith is like the electric company - it gives power at all times. Faith kicks in when the lights go out; when the doctors give you up, and you begin to pray, kick in faith power.

Faith is a rider and will ride out all the odds! It is visible. It moves in silence and in the blind. It can become a silent killer to everything that is coming up against you! We must know when the devil comes up against us to destroy everything. We are going to come out winning every time. Faith is like a time clock; keep on watching it because God, His timing is always perfect. Your faith is blind, so keep watching Him and claim it is yours. God is going to show up for you and show out if only you keep on believing. In God, you have everything you need.

A mother, father, sister, brother, or friend cannot compare. Faith is not something God will come down from heaven and motivate you to have—it is something we have to motivate ourselves with, and without it, we cannot please God.

Faith is so important to have in your everyday walk of life. I cannot imagine life without faith; for me, it is the easiest walk of life. Faith takes you places that your money cannot buy you. Faith is not up for sale; you cannot purchase it. Faith requires that you believe it, trust it, and live it. Faith is so great that God made it according to what we are willing to believe. Starting off with a grain, even if that is enough to move mountains, it is still connected to a system called your belief system and works according to what you are willing to believe. Faith is an eye-opener; it will make people automatically change their minds about a lot of things. Faith reaches God in ways your prayers cannot reach Him because FAITH is the only way you can please God. According to God's word, it is impossible to please Him without it. God needs you to believe and trust Him wholeheartedly, not halfway, but all the way. Your FAITH has to be in alignment with God for it to work. There are many different ranks of faith:

1. General

2. Captain

3. Soldier

4. Warrior

5. Dimensional

6. Level

7. Mustard seed

Faith is a system that cannot and will not be broken; only God can block or stop your faith. This system cannot be stolen from you but can be blocked if you allow negativity to set in. When we doubt God, faith cannot operate. In life, you have to be willing to jump with your faith. Even if the people and loved ones around you are not willing to jump, that is fine! God just needs you to jump! Your movement means that you are tired of sitting back and doing nothing about your situation and, therefore, are deciding to jump. Go for it no matter what man has to say.

Whose report are you going to believe? I am going to believe the report of the Lord! God's report says that I can do all things through Christ who strengthens me (Philippians 4:13). His report says I am free. His report says by His stripes I am healed! His report says that I have not because I ask not. In other words, God's report simply tells me that I have to jump! If I am planning on having a win in my life, faith can and will chase away doubt if I believe. Remember this nugget:

Your faith can be tied up if you are always around negative people.

Faith is like a jumper cable - it can be boosted with a jump start. That is the only way it is going to fire up. Once your faith gets a boost, you will begin to feel like you are charged and ready to take on the world. You will begin feeling like you can conquer anything and anybody. Your faith has to be pushed in order to receive a fresh wind. Your faith has levels to it, which can be developed through staying in the fight that is within you to win. Faith cancels out fear. No matter what, your faith can be so powerful that it overrides all your "not approved" statuses. Faith is a purchaser, but it cannot be purchased. God passes it out for free according to our faith measurements, which we all were born with.

The day the doctor says it is a boy or a girl, we came into this world by faith. God is looking for some generational curse breakers through faith who are not afraid to jump in this season and who are going to decree and declare that the curse is broken over their families, whether it be drugs, prostitution, crack, liars, cheaters, killers, or diseases. The curse is broken through FAITH; we will not be cursed with depression or oppression, but instead, we are going to take a leap of faith and jump out of this situation. We as a people have to have enough faith to believe that we can and will defeat and press through. Live through it no matter what it looks like despite the loss. If you are still breathing, you have to believe God will always have a way of escape for you through faith. Have you ever sat down and said to yourself, "Why does God allow so many obstacles to come our way or to come up against us?" Take a moment and think about it. We have to step out in faith; God takes the foolish things to confound the wise. We would not have a need for faith if we did not go through things or if there were no obstacles to overcome. I thank God for developing such a great blessing to help us reach our goals. Faith is blinded and cannot be seen. You can only hope for it through your belief system. Faith can only be issued by God.

CHAPTER 8

Period

This book of faith can help take you to a deep place in your faith walk with the Lord; it will make you or break you down. Many people go around thinking that they are working miracles; they have made so much money in a lifetime, but they had great faith. They pay their tithes and abide by God's laws that allow them to be blessed. God blesses the just and the unjust if they obey His word. Some believe that because people are out in the world, God will not bless them. Not so! Stop saying that the world looks like they are being blessed and that we are not! We are having faith the way God has instructed! It appears that the saints are suffering, and the world looks blessed. Yes, some people in the world are blessed because even though they have a worldly life, some obey God more than we do. When it comes to being faithful, the only problem is that they are not in church. They are committing sinful acts, but we, as people of God, do the same thing when we do not obey God's word. That is why Matthew 7 says, "Judge not, for you will not be judged."

God knew none of us would be able to point the finger.

We are all like flowers in God's eyesight, and if you want to know what type of flower you are in faith, study your seed. It will allow you to know what you are growing. When you study who you really are and have faith enough to do a study on yourself, a lot of people's problems are the reason you do not have faith enough to step out and reap the harvest. Some of you are in your thirties, forties, and even fifties and are still angry and holding grudges from grade school. Maybe your sisters or brothers have got fewer whippings than you. In your mind, you could not understand why because you felt like you were not that bad, but once you study your seed, you might realize that a lot of stuff you are going through now is because of all the childhood stuff you did. Maybe you are stuck on your high school or college days and find yourself still reaping what you sowed. Just because it looks like you got away and did not go to jail when you should have, you did not get away with God. Your faith should be able to sustain you in your time of need. Faith is one of life's most powerful tools when it is in God and not a man. We can trust God with our lives and be broken at the same time. Ask God to show you how to do things His way and help you not repeat the same mistakes. Talk to God and ask Him for His guidance. You have to open up your heart if you are going to hear from God. David did a lot of wrong in the bible, yet God said he was a man after His own heart because his faith and prayers touched God.

    As sons and daughters of God, we must lift up standards in God's word and our faith. We go through so much because we are so afraid to step out in faith without money. We have to ask the Lord to deliver us! If you are struggling with your past, just say, "Oh God! Deliver me!" "Now faith is the substance of things hoped for and the evidence of things not seen. For by it the elders obtained a good report through faith we understand that the world was framed by the word of God. So that things which are seen were not made of things which do appear. By faith,

Abel offered unto God a more excellent sacrifice than Cain, by which he obtained witness the he was righteous, God testifying of his gifts and by faith Enoch was translated that he should not see death and was not found because God had translated him before his translation he had this testimony, that he please God. But without faith it is impossible to please Him, for he that cometh to God must believe that he is, and he is a rewarder of them that diligently seek Him. By faith Noah, being warned of God of things not seen as yet moved with fear, prepared an ark to the saving of his house by which he condemned the world and became heir of the righteousness which is by faith. By faith Abraham, when was called to go out into a place which he should after receive for an inheritance, obeyed and he went out knowing whither he went?

    By faith he sojourned in the land of promise, as in a strange country, dwelling in tabernacle with Isaac and Jacob, the heirs with him of the same promise. For he looked for a city which hate foundation whose builder and maker is God. Through faith also Sara herself received strength to conceive seed delivered a child when she was past age because she judged him faithful. Who had promised? Therefore, sprang there even one, and him as good as dead so many as the stars of the sky in multitude

And as the sand which is by the seashore innumerable. These all died in faith, not having received the promises but having seen them afar off and embraced them and confessed that they were strangers and pilgrims on the earth.

                                        Hebrews 11:1-13

As people of God, we have to remember to not fake it until we make it! That is garbage advice; FACE it until you make it get up. Work hard. If you fall, stand back up and face it again. Once you do a little better, if you fail again, get back up. The Bible declares that a young man will fall seven times but has to get back up. The easy part was the fall; the hard part was getting back up. If this were not a true statement, people worldwide would be able to get back up right away. People will know that they have a right to repent 77 times, 77 per day. We fall every time we doubt God or say God cannot do something. We do not see it like that because maybe we are faithful to our local church or faithful to our pastors. We can become faithful to reading God's Word or faithful to prayer. Still, when it comes to trusting God or having faith in God, we have this big black light up, as though we do not know for sure if we should trust or depend on God because the love people have for money has messed them up. The Bible says that the love of money is the root of all evil. This is true because the "money system" has messed up people's eyesight. I believe this is why a lot of people like to use the saying, "God gave us common sense." Do not get me wrong, that is an absolutely true statement — God gives us common sense in the natural world. Still, He also gives blinded sense in the spiritual walk. Common sense could not even comprehend nor compare itself with FAITH. This is believing in what your common sense cannot and will not detect and will outdo any amount of money you can ever receive in your lifetime. It is also connected to favor, which comes straight from God. Common sense does not even see God doing it. Your common sense will tell you that you are crazy for leaving that job and believing that God is going to take care of you. Common sense will tell you, "Why are you waiting on God for a husband? You better go get you a man!" You have to understand that the devil is involved in common sense.

He controls the common world, but God's word overrides the common world every time. Your common sense cannot be used to compare. Yes, it sounds foolish that common sense would not give you enough sense to know that money could stand next to your faith. Money can pay some bills, and yes, it can get you nice things and a nice bank account balance, but your faith can take you places your money cannot get you nor buy you. Your faith is connected to your future. It covers you and what is connected to you. Look at it like this — it is your deposit into your heavenly bank accounts every time you step out. Have FAITH, pray, and trust in God's words. You are making deposits that common sense would not give. You do not even have a clue what is happening in the spiritual realm when you step out. God's word says that without faith, it is impossible to please God. I advise you, people of God, to start activating your faith, step out into the blind, pray, and trust God with it, and you will begin to enter into your new outlook on life. If you are going to use common sense, use it to believe that

God is all-powerful and omnipotent, the beginning and the ending of everything and everyone.

I pray and hope and trust that after reading this book it encourages you all to do something different in your life and to step out with the level of faith that you can believe God on. He loves us all and has no respect of person. He loves us all the same; there are no "big I's and little u's" when it comes to God. That is why He says the first will be last, and the last will be first. That said, you are still here in the land of the living; if you have never grabbed hold of faith like this, decide to do it today.

Lord, I pray a special blessing over the one reading this book. I pray that their faith will be built up in You. Whatever they hope for, let their faith be ignited right here right now! As they reflect on this book, cause them to understand that FAITH in You is the real game changer in their walk with You. All they need is a grain.

Be blessed! I hope and pray that your family will be blessed also. I decree and declare that everything connected to me will be blessed from this day forward.

If this book has been a blessing to you, I want to encourage you to email me at global.move@yahoo.com to set up an appointment and become a part of my Facebook community. We would love to hear from you!

Connect with the Author

Dr. Cherie Owens—Sims was born and raised in Milwaukee, Wisconsin, to her proud parents, the late Marshall and Emma Owens. In November 2011, Sims received her master's in Christian counseling and doctorate in Divinity at Agape Bible College in Milwaukee, Wisconsin. Seven months later, Dr. Sims graced the stage once again at MATC, receiving her diploma as an educator for cosmetology. Dr. Sims is an anointed woman of God. She is a world-renowned Prophetess who moves in the mantle of her mother's constant declaration, "God has never failed me yet!"

Dr. Cherie is married to the love of her life, Elder Lyndon Sims, who serves as her number one pusher along with her children and grandchildren. Her family wholeheartedly believes in and supports what God has called her to do. She is a great wife, mother, grandmother, mother-in-law, daughter, friend, and so much more. Dr. Sims attends World Shakers Church, the ER, as the Associate Pastor under the leadership of Apostle Dennis Spears and Pastor Lakesha Spears. She founded Increase Salon, Increase Your Faith Bootcamp, and Increase Designs.

She owned fourteen salons, a beauty supply store, and a significant daycare (Tweedy and Tots Academy), and she was blessed to mentor fifteen academies in Milwaukee, WI. In conjunction with her ministerial mantle, Dr. Sims is also a life coach and a playwright preparing to take her plays on the road. She is not mentioning this to brag but to show you that when life throws you a curve ball, she proves you can take a lick and keep ticking. She has gracefully embraced her trials and tribulations and now hosts an International Movement; she smiles and mentors' men and women to walk out what they have been through into your new.

Right when I thought I was going to quit, God brought me to a new platform, the "clubhouse." That is when God officially allowed me to embrace the international anointing that is on my life. Despite her many hats, she applies God's Word and balance to it all!

Made in the USA
Columbia, SC
27 March 2025